HEALTHY SNACKS

CLAUDIA MARTIN

Enslow Publishing
101 W. 23rd Street
Suite 240
New York, NY 10011
USA

enslow.com

Published in 2019 by Enslow Publishing, LLC.
101 W. 23rd Street, Suite 240, New York, NY 10011

Editors: Sarah Eason and Jennifer Sanderson
Designers: Paul Myerscough and Simon Borrough
Picture Researcher: Claudia Martin

Cataloging-in-Publication Data
Names: Martin, Claudia.
Title: Healthy snacks / Claudia Martin.
Description: New York : Enslow Publishing, 2019. | Series: Cooking skills | Includes glossary and index.
Identifiers: ISBN 9781978506657 (pbk.) | ISBN 9781978506381 (library bound) | ISBN 9781978506329 (ebook)
Subjects: LCSH: Snack foods—Juvenile literature. | Nutrition—Juvenile literature. | Cookbooks—Juvenile literature.
Classification: LCC TX740.M35 2019 | DDC 642—dc23

Printed in the United States of America

To Our Readers: We have done our best to make sure all website addresses in this book were active and appropriate when we went to press. However, the author and the publisher have no control over and assume no liability for the material available on those websites or on any websites they may link to. Any comments or suggestions can be sent by e-mail to customerservice@enslow.com.

Photo Credits: Cover: Shutterstock: gosphotodesign: br; Kaspars Grinvalds: bl; margouillat photo: tc; nenetus: bc. Inside: Shutterstock: 2xSamara.com: p.17t; Africa Studio: p.44t; Aleksandr Markin: pp.16–17; Aleksandrs Samuilovs: p.39t; Amalia Ferreira Espinoza: pp.30–31; Andrey Smirnov: pp.1r, 34t; Anna Hoychuk: pp.38–39; Anna Shepulova: pp.10–11; Anna_Pustynnikova: p.24l; Anton Albert: pp.40, 46; Ariwasabi: p.1l; bbernard: p.20; Blend Images: p.32; Botamochy: p.33r; Brent Hofacker: pp.21tr, 26–27, 36–37, 46–47, 48; Cesarz: pp.12–13; CGissemann: p.18t; Daisy Daisy: pp.34–35; Daxiao Productions: p.10l; Dean Drobot: pp.40–41; Dejan Stanic Micko: p.29; Djero Adlibeshe: p.14l; Elena Schweitzer: p.34b; Evgeny Karandaev: p.27tr; exousia: p.12cl; Fascinadora: p.45; GCapture: p.21tc; goodmoments: p.42b; HandmadePictures: p.27tl; Ilkiv Anastasia: pp.28–29; Imcsike: p.37b; inewsfoto: p.10r; Irina Rostokina: p.41; Ivana Lalicki: pp.18–19; Jacob Lund: p.12tr; Jiri Hera: p.42c; KPG Ivary: pp.6–7; Lapina Maria: pp.14–15; lenetstan: p.27cr; margouillat photo: pp.2–3, 44–45; Maridav: p.37t; Martin Novak: p.30t; Michelle Lee Photography: p.19; MJTH: pp.8–9; Monkey Business Images: p.7; MRProduction: p.14r; Myvisuals: p.18b; Nataliya Arzamasova: pp.4, 32–33; nenetus: p.42t; Olexandr Panchenko: p.24r; Patrick T. Power: p.5; Paul Cowan: pp.24–25; ProStockStudio: p.23; RossHelen: p.39b; R Szatkowski: pp.20–21; Samuel Borges Photography: p.22; SL: pp.22–23; SMDSS: p.30b; Solis Images: p.44b; StockLite: pp.4–5; tacar: pp.42–43; takayuki: p.33l; Thanthima Lim: p.38; Wayhome Studio: p.17b.

CONTENTS

CHAPTER 1

GET COOKING!

Between tests and sports, it is easy to work up an appetite. If you want a snack, should you grab a bag of chips or make one of these delicious recipes?

Should You Snack?

Growing children and teens need to keep their energy levels stable, particularly in that late-afternoon time when tempers can be frayed and concentration dips. Most nutritionists suggest that teens eat three healthy meals and one small, healthy snack per day. You can increase that to two snacks if you are very active.

The Wrong Kind of Snacks

The problem with snacking is that most people grab something they know will give them a quick energy boost—that is often potato chips, cookies, chocolate, or other foods high in salt, sugar, or saturated fats. Saturated fats, found in meat and dairy products, are the "bad" fats that can lead to heart disease.

A healthy and energy-giving snack contains a small portion of low-fat protein and a small portion of fiber-rich fruit, vegetables, nuts, seeds, or whole grains. Nuts, seeds, beans, lean meat, fish, and low-fat yogurt are good sources of protein. Whole grains are found in whole wheat bread, oats, and other unrefined cereals, which have not been processed to remove the fiber- and nutrient-rich germ (kernel) and bran (outer layer). The carbohydrates from whole grains are absorbed more slowly into your bloodstream, keeping your energy levels stable.

Store It Up

As you look through the snack suggestions in this book, you will notice that some ingredients appear many times. If you keep these staple ingredients in your pantry or refrigerator, you will always be able to grab a healthy snack when you need it:

- Whole wheat bread or flour
- Fresh fruit
- Dried fruit
- Fresh vegetables
- Nuts
- Seeds
- Low-fat yogurt
- Vegetable oil
- Spices and herbs

5

READ THE RECIPE...

Itching to make a snack? The first step is to choose a recipe that you will enjoy.

Make Your Choice

When choosing a recipe, think about how much time you have to prepare your snack. Also consider who you are feeding—just yourself, your family, or a dozen friends? If you have plenty of time, turn to Chapter 2 to fry up pancakes. If you are hungry and need carbohydrates, try the breads in Chapter 3. The salads in Chapter 4 are perfect for snacks or a light family lunch. The baked goods in Chapter 5 need a little more preparation, but will delight any gathering. For quick nut and seed recipes, flick to Chapter 6. Or turn to Chapter 7 for creative ideas with fruit.

How Much, How Hot?

In this book, measurements are given in ounces (oz), followed by grams (g), as well as cups, followed by milliliters (ml). There are 240 ml in each cup. Sometimes, you will be told to add a teaspoon (tsp) or tablespoon (tbsp) of an ingredient. There are 5 ml in each teaspoon and 15 ml in each tablespoon. When a "pinch" or a "sprinkle" is suggested, the exact amount is not that important—but go easy on the cayenne pepper!

Oven temperatures are given in Fahrenheit (°F), followed by Celsius (°C). When cooking on a stove, if you do not know how hot to turn the ring, go for a low heat, then turn it up if the cooking is taking longer than the recipe suggests.

Buy Ingredients

When you have chosen a recipe, figure out which ingredients you need to buy, and which equipment you need to use. Most of the recipes serve four people as a snack, so multiply or divide as needed. Some recipes, such as the baked goods in Chapter 5 and the nut mixes in Chapter 6, make bigger quantities but they can be stored in an airtight container until needed. Remember that some ingredients keep for months (like flour and cooking oil), while others need to be bought a day or two before use (like fresh herbs and salad leaves).

Create Your Snack

Although the recipes in this book are quick and simple, always overestimate how long it will take to make them, so you are not still whisking the batter when your friends want pancakes. Read the recipe instructions carefully, before cracking the eggs. The ingredients are listed in the order they are used, which should help you not to leave out anything. If you want to brush up on your cooking skills before you begin, take a look at the "Mastering the Basics" sections at the start of each chapter.

...OR GO YOUR OWN WAY

Treat these recipes as guidelines—
then let loose your creativity!

Test It Out

The first time you cook one of these snacks, play it safe by following the instructions closely and measuring the ingredients exactly. Then, as you sample your creations, ask yourself—and your friends—what is good or not so good about the flavors, textures, and colors. Is the bruschetta too garlicky? Would you rather spit out the raisins? Would you prefer your nuts more subtle than spicy? The "Chef's Tip" box beside each recipe might offer ideas for adding different spices or flavorings. Also take a look at the "Switch It Up" boxes at the beginning of each chapter, which offer additional ideas for ingredient changes and other healthy combinations.

Special Diets

If you will be offering your snacks to vegetarian friends, or you are vegetarian yourself, all of the recipes are meat- and fish-free—except for the salads in Chapter 4. Check out the "Switch It Up" sections for vegetarian options. To make the recipes vegan, you will need to switch honey, eggs, and cheese or other dairy products for vegan alternatives. Be sure to ask your friends if they have food intolerances and allergies. In particular, remember that nut and seed allergies are common and potentially very serious. In the case of a gluten allergy, flours made from other grains, roots, and legumes are often gluten-free and so labeled.

Keep It Clean

Before you start to make a snack, remember these hygiene rules:

- Wash your hands with soap and warm water.
- Make sure your work surfaces and equipment are clean.
- If you have long hair, tie it back.
- Wash fruit and vegetables under cold running water, even if you plan on peeling them.
- When working with raw meat or fish, wash your hands after handling, and use a different cutting board and knife from the one for other ingredients.
- Never serve undercooked meat, fish, or eggs—make sure there is no pink meat, that fish is firm all the way through, and eggs are not runny.
- Check the use-by dates on all ingredients.
- Do not leave food out of the refrigerator for more than two hours.

CHAPTER 2

PANCAKES

Maybe pancakes do not always spring to mind when you think of healthy snacks, but if made with the right ingredients, pancakes can be nutritious, filling, and delicious.

Top Toppings

The reason why many pancakes are not top of the healthy list is their toppings! When you slather pancakes in maple syrup or butter, you are adding a lot of calories and a high dose of either sugar or saturated fat. So stick to healthier toppings, such as stewed or fresh fruit, and try not to add too much sugar or salt to your batter.

Making Good Choices

If you make your pancakes with whole wheat flour, you are providing a dose of energy-giving carbohydrates, fiber, and nutrients. The egg and any butter in pancake mix do contain saturated fat, but they also contain protein. Keep that saturated fat to a healthier level by frying pancakes in oils that are low in saturates, such as canola, corn, or sunflower oil. All in all, pancakes can make a healthy snack, as long as you eat them in moderation.

Whole Wheat Pancake Batter

Knowing how to make pancake batter is a useful skill. Knowing how to make it from whole wheat flour is an even more useful one. Here is how to make enough batter for four pancakes:

1 In a large bowl, mix together ¾ cup (100 g) whole wheat all-purpose flour with ½ tbsp baking powder and a pinch of salt. For sweet pancakes, you could add a little sugar. Set aside.

2 Crack 1 egg into a cup, then beat with a fork.

3 In another bowl, whisk together ½ the egg (keep the other half for an omelette), ¾ cup (180 ml) milk, and 2 tbsp melted butter or margarine.

4 Make a well in the center of the flour, then pour in the milk mixture.

5 Stir with a fork until well combined. If the batter is extremely thick, add 1 tbsp milk to thin, test, and add more if necessary.

Switch It Up

If you enjoy the pancakes on page 12, but would rather not top them with applesauce, try these alternatives: to make a berry compote topping, put 1½ cups (200 g) of frozen mixed berries in a saucepan with a little water and simmer gently for five to eight minutes until softened. Or try the no-cook option of low-fat plain yogurt and sliced mango.

PANCAKES WITH APPLESAUCE

This delicious applesauce has no added sugar—the apples are sweet enough without it.

Filling, sweet, and surprisingly healthy!

You Will Need

2 lb (900 g) apples
¼ cup (60 ml) water
1 tsp ground cinnamon
Whole wheat batter for four pancakes
   (see page 11)
1–2 tbsp canola oil

Instructions

1 Peel, core, and cube your apples.
2 Put the apples in a saucepan along with the water and cinnamon.
3 Cover with a lid and cook over a medium heat for twenty minutes, until the apples are very soft. Check regularly that the apples are not drying out or sticking to the pan. Set your applesauce to one side.
4 Make your pancake batter using the recipe on page 11.
5 Heat a little canola oil in a frying pan or skillet.
6 Put 3 to 4 tbsp of batter onto the pan. Spread it into a 4-inch (10 cm) circle, using the back of a spoon if necessary.
7 After about two minutes, the pancake should be bubbling a little and the edges should be dry and curling away from the side of the pan. Flip over the pancake with a spatula, then fry for about two minutes on the other side, until golden and cooked through. Repeat for the other three pancakes.
8 Serve your pancakes with dollops of applesauce.

CHEF'S TIP

For a richer flavor, add ½ tsp of vanilla extract to your batter before cooking.

GREEN PANCAKES

This recipe makes four sumptuous spinach pancakes, perfect for snacks, breakfast, and any other time.

spinach

You Will Need

4 oz (115 g) spinach
Boiling water
½ egg, beaten
⅔ cup (160 ml) low-fat buttermilk
¾ cup (100 g) whole wheat flour
½ tsp baking powder
Pinch of salt
1–2 tbsp canola oil

Instructions

1. Put the washed spinach in a colander in the sink, then carefully pour boiling water over it to wilt it. Squeeze out all the water, then pat dry with paper towels.
2. Use a food processor or hand-held blender to puree your spinach, or chop it for a chunkier texture.
3. Mix together the spinach, egg, and buttermilk in a jug or small bowl.
4. In a large mixing bowl, combine the flour, baking powder, and salt. Gradually pour in the buttermilk mixture, stirring until fully combined. Add a little water or buttermilk if the mixture is very thick.
5. Heat a little canola oil in a frying pan or skillet.
6. Put 3 or 4 tbsp of batter onto the skillet for your first pancake. Spread it into a 4-inch (10 cm) circle, using the back of a spoon if the consistency is thick.
7. After about two minutes, bubbles should appear and the edges of the pancake should dry and lift off the pan. Flip over with a spatula, then fry for one to two minutes on the other side, until golden. Repeat for the other pancakes.

What a great way to eat your greens.

CHEF'S TIP

Add a pinch of paprika to the pancake batter for a bit of spice!

CHAPTER 3
BREADS

Whether it comes in the form of toast, sandwiches, or freshly baked rolls, bread is a classic choice for a snack. Best of all, bread can be combined with healthy spreads and fillings.

Filling Food

Bread makes a great snack because it offers energy-boosting carbohydrates. Whenever possible, choose whole grain bread—or bake your bread with whole grain flour—because it contains more fiber and nutrients, and will keep your energy levels stable for longer.

Something Extra

To really satisfy your hunger, add a little low-fat protein to your snack, putting it inside your sandwich or bagel, or layering it on your toast or bruschetta. A common choice of protein is peanut butter, but other healthy options include fish, hummus, low-fat cheese, or lean meats, such as turkey.

Switch It Up

Although tomato bruschetta is the classic choice (see the recipe on page 20), there are plenty of other choices for bruschetta toppings. Try experimenting with cream cheese, smoked salmon, and a squeeze of lemon. How about topping your bread with sliced avocado and sun-dried tomatoes? Or try chopped tomatoes, mozzarella, and canned anchovy fillets.

Mastering the Basics
Kneading Dough

Why does bread dough need kneading? When flour and water are combined, proteins in the flour expand to form strands of gluten. Kneading warms and stretches the strands, so that when the yeast, or other raising agent, makes the bread rise, the strands will hold little pockets of carbon dioxide gas. Without kneading, bread would be flat and tough. Here is how to knead bread dough:

1. Dust a clean surface with a little flour to keep the dough from sticking.
2. Put the ball of dough onto the surface, then squash it with the heel of your hand, pushing it away from you to stretch it. Do not be too gentle: make sure you give the dough a good stretch.
3. Pull the dough back into a ball, give it a quarter turn, and repeat.
4. Keep kneading and turning for at least ten minutes.
5. To test if the dough is ready, pull a piece from the ball, then stretch it into a sheet. If you can pull the dough thin enough to see sunlight through it, your work is done.

OLIVE BREAD

Follow this simple recipe to bake eight crusty-on-the-outside, squishy-on-the-inside rolls.

black olives

Fill your kitchen with the scent of the Mediterranean!

You Will Need

1 cup (125 g) whole wheat bread flour
1 cup (125 g) plain bread flour
1 tsp salt
½ tsp sugar
1 tsp yeast
⅔ cup (160 ml) warm water
2 tbsp olive oil
Handful of pitted black olives
Sprig of fresh rosemary

Instructions

1 In a large mixing bowl, stir together the flour, salt, sugar, and yeast.
2 Chop the olives. Pick the leaves from the rosemary stem, then chop them finely. Stir the olives and rosemary into the flour mixture.
3 Make a well in the center of the flour. Pour in the water and 1 tbsp olive oil. Mix until you have a sticky, dough-like consistency.
4 Dust a clean counter with flour, then knead the dough on it. Turn to page 17 to find out how to knead.
5 Put the dough back in the mixing bowl, cover with a clean towel, and leave in a warm place for one hour.
6 Around fifteen minutes before the end of the hour, preheat the oven to 445°F (230°C).
7 Cover a baking sheet with parchment paper or aluminum foil.
8 Divide the dough into eight balls, lightly brush them with 1 tbsp olive oil, then place them on the tray.
9 Bake in the oven for ten minutes, until golden brown.

yeast

CHEF'S TIP

If you like sun-dried tomatoes, add 1 oz (30 g) of them, chopped into small pieces, to your dough.

19

TOMATO BRUSCHETTA

For a dose of energy-giving carbohydrates and vitamin C, rustle up these pretty bruschettas.

You Will Need

4 medium tomatoes, chopped
1 garlic clove, peeled and finely sliced
1 tbsp chopped fresh parsley
1 tbsp balsamic vinegar
2 tbsp olive oil
Salt and pepper
1 ciabatta or ½ French baguette

Instructions

1 In a bowl, mix together the tomatoes, garlic, and parsley. Reserve a little parsley for garnishing.
2 Pour in the balsamic vinegar and olive oil, then season with salt and pepper.
3 Place the tomato mix in the refrigerator for one hour, to give the flavors time to blend.
4 Cut the bread into thick slices, then lightly brown them in a toaster or under a broiler.
5 Spread each slice with the tomato mixture, then sprinkle with parsley.

Invite some friends over to enjoy this Italian snack.

CHAPTER 4

SALADS

Everyone knows salads are good for you—and they can also be exciting. Read on for enticing ways to eat your greens.

Pack in Protein

If you feel like a snack, you should eat something that will fill you up a little, at least until your next meal. A few lettuce leaves will not do the trick. The key to making a salad to boost your energy levels is to add a little protein and some carbohydrates. In the Caesar Salad on page 26, protein comes in the form of chicken and grated cheese. In the Salad Nicoise, the protein is the tuna, anchovies, and egg. Other protein options for salads include beans, nuts, and seeds.

Include Carbohydrates

Carbohydrates, particularly those that feature whole grains, will keep you fueled for longer. Consider adding new potatoes, pasta, or a sprinkling of croutons to your salads. Another alternative is to serve your salad with a side of whole grain bread.

Switch It Up

The simplest salads contain just one main ingredient, such as grated carrot or sliced ripe tomatoes dressed in vinaigrette. Throw some chopped cilantro leaves and toasted sesame seeds in with the carrot for a zingier taste. Or add some Greek feta cheese to those tomatoes for a salty-sweet flavor.

Mastering the Basics
Vinaigrette

A salad can taste dull without dressing, such as vinaigrette. Vinaigrettes are usually mixtures of oil and vinegar, but an equal mixture will be too sharp—go for roughly three spoons of oil to every spoon of vinegar. The oil and vinegar will separate within minutes, unless you add an extra ingredient, called an emulsifier, to hold them together. In this recipe, the emulsifier is mustard. Here is how to make about ⅔ of a cup (160 ml) of vinaigrette:

1 In a small bowl, mix together ½ tsp salt, 1 tsp Dijon mustard, and 2 tbsp white wine vinegar.

2 Add 6 tbsp olive oil and whisk with a fork.

3 Drizzle over your salad, then toss.

SALAD NICOISE

This classic French salad originated in the city of Nice—that is how it got its name.

Grab a fork and get started!

green beans

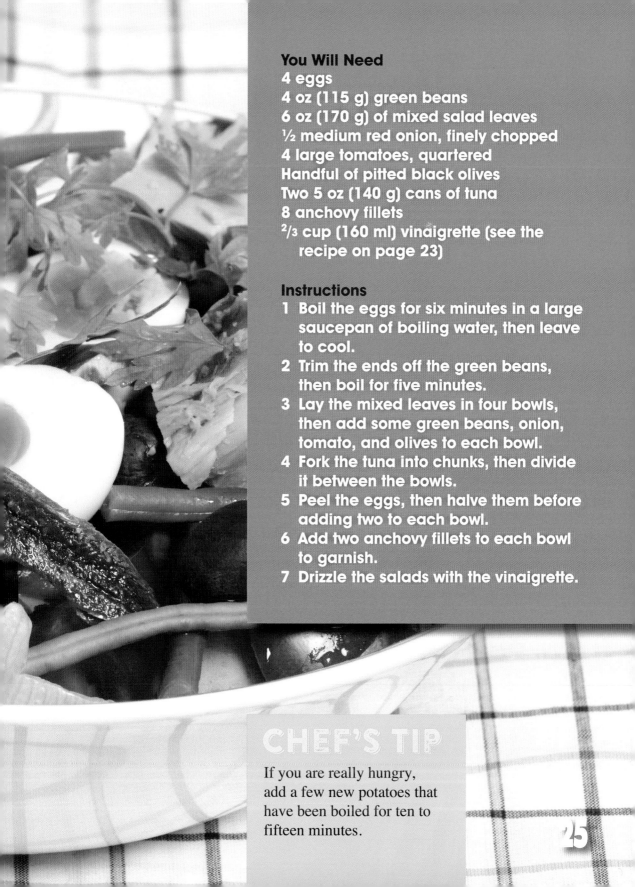

You Will Need
4 eggs
4 oz (115 g) green beans
6 oz (170 g) of mixed salad leaves
½ medium red onion, finely chopped
4 large tomatoes, quartered
Handful of pitted black olives
Two 5 oz (140 g) cans of tuna
8 anchovy fillets
⅔ cup (160 ml) vinaigrette (see the
   recipe on page 23)

Instructions
1 Boil the eggs for six minutes in a large saucepan of boiling water, then leave to cool.
2 Trim the ends off the green beans, then boil for five minutes.
3 Lay the mixed leaves in four bowls, then add some green beans, onion, tomato, and olives to each bowl.
4 Fork the tuna into chunks, then divide it between the bowls.
5 Peel the eggs, then halve them before adding two to each bowl.
6 Add two anchovy fillets to each bowl to garnish.
7 Drizzle the salads with the vinaigrette.

CHEF'S TIP

If you are really hungry, add a few new potatoes that have been boiled for ten to fifteen minutes.

CAESAR SALAD

Invented by Italian-American chef Caesar Cardini, this salad is a favorite for a good reason.

You Will Need
4 tbsp mayonnaise
Juice of 1 lemon
2 tsp Dijon mustard
5 tbsp Parmesan cheese, grated
Salt and pepper
1 head of romaine lettuce
1 cup (40 g) ready-made croutons
6 oz (170 g) cooked chicken,
    chopped or ripped

Instructions
1 Whisk together the mayonnaise, lemon juice, mustard, and 4 tbsp of the Parmesan cheese. Season with a little salt and pepper.
2 Tear or cut the lettuce into strips and chunks, then lay it on four plates.
3 Drizzle the dressing over the lettuce.
4 Sprinkle the croutons on, then place the chicken on the salad.
5 Before serving, sprinkle with the remaining Parmesan.

Parmesan cheese

A delicious classic!

If you are just serving
yourself, remember to divide
the measurements by four.

CHAPTER 5
BAKED GOODS

Baking is always fun—and the results will make you popular with friends and family.

Pick Your Ingredients

Can baked goods ever be considered healthy? The issue with many store-bought baked goods is that they are made with refined flour, saturated fats (such as those in butter), and refined sugar. The recipes in this chapter use whole grain flour and as little saturated fat as possible. One way to reduce saturated fat in baked goods is to switch butter for an unsaturated spread suitable for baking. In addition, these recipes are sweetened with natural sugars, such as honey and fruit. Honey will give less of a sugar rush than refined sugar, but it is still high in calories, so use it in moderation.

Bake to Share

With a careful choice of ingredients, baked goods can make an appearance in a balanced diet. Any sweet baked treats will be relatively high in calories, so do not keep your baked goods to yourself—share them with whoever is quick enough to grab them.

Mastering the Basics
Rising

The recipe on page 30 calls for both baking soda and baking powder. Why use both and what do they actually do? It is very useful for a baker to know exactly how these raising agents work:

1 Baking soda (which is also known as bicarbonate of soda) creates a chemical reaction when mixed with something acidic, such as yogurt, buttermilk, honey, maple syrup, brown sugar, fruit juices, or chocolate. The reaction creates bubbles of carbon dioxide, which make the mixture "rise" in the oven.

2 Baking powder is baking soda already mixed with something acidic, so it can be used in recipes without acidic ingredients. The powder stays "inert," or nonreactive, until mixed with a liquid, when it creates bubbles.

3 Why use both powder and soda if they do the same job? Not all recipes use both, but if your recipe already contains acidic ingredients, using baking powder on its own can make your baked goods taste acidic. Since baking soda is less powerful than baking powder, using soda alone might not give the lift you need.

Switch It Up

If you enjoy the oat bars on page 32, it is easy to customize the recipe. Just swap the blueberries for different fruits, such as raspberries or raisins. If you feel like treating yourself, use chocolate chips and desiccated coconut instead. You could leave out the fruit and just add a pinch of ground ginger to the mix.

CARROT MUFFINS

Bake twelve of these sweetly spiced but far-from-unhealthy muffins.

grated carrot

Sweetened only with honey!

You Will Need

1 cup (110 g) carrots
1 cup (125 g) whole wheat flour
½ tsp baking soda
½ tsp baking powder
½ tsp cinnamon
Pinch of ground ginger
3 tbsp honey
1 small egg, beaten
4 tbsp plain yogurt
3 tbsp margarine, softened
½ tsp vanilla essence

Instructions

1 Preheat the oven to 400°F (200°C). Place twelve paper baking cups in a muffin tray.
2 Grate your carrots.
3 In a large bowl, mix together the dry ingredients: flour, baking soda, baking powder, cinnamon, and ginger.
4 In another bowl, stir together the carrots, honey, egg, yogurt, margarine, and vanilla essence.
5 Now combine the wet and dry ingredients, stirring until mixed.
6 Spoon the mixture into your baking cups, then bake for fifteen minutes until golden.

CHEF'S TIP

For extra sweetness, add
4 tbsp of raisins in Step 3.

BLUEBERRY OAT BARS

These oat bars will be gobbled up in an instant!

You Will Need
7 tbsp margarine
5 tbsp runny honey
1¾ cups (175 g) rolled oats
¼ cup (30 g) whole wheat flour
¾ cup (100 g) blueberries

Instructions
1 Preheat the oven to 350°F (180°C).
  Line an 8-inch (20-cm) square baking pan
  with parchment paper.
2 Melt the margarine in a small saucepan,
  then pour into a mixing bowl.
3 Add the honey and stir until mixed well.
4 Stir in the oats, flour, and blueberries.
5 Press the mixture into the baking pan.
6 Bake for eighteen to twenty-two minutes,
  until golden brown.
7 Cut into squares, then leave to cool on the
  baking sheet.
8 Eat when cool but if you want to save the
  bars, they will keep for a couple of days
  in a tightly sealed container, or in the
  refrigerator for a little longer.

CHEF'S TIP

If your bars are crumbly once they are cooled, put them in the refrigerator for one hour or overnight to firm up.

Filling, fruity, and fabulous!

CHAPTER 6

NUTS AND SEEDS

Nuts and seeds make great energy-boosting snacks. Just make sure to ask your friends about nut and seed allergies before serving these.

Nutritious Nuts!

Nuts are nutritional super-foods. They are loaded with protein, unsaturated fats, fiber, vitamins, and minerals. They are high in calories, so do not overload on them. However, snacking on nuts is very satisfying, so you may find you do not crave sugary treats for a while afterward. Store-bought nuts are often high in added sugar and salt, so roast your own or—best of all—eat them raw. Popular snacking nuts include peanuts, almonds, cashews, Brazil nuts, pecans, pistachios, macadamias, and walnuts.

Super Seeds!

Like nuts, seeds are also nutritious. Tasty and healthy seeds include sunflower, pumpkin, squash, sesame, flax, hemp, and chia. Seeds can be eaten raw, toasted, or mixed into granola, oatmeal, salads, and smoothies.

Toasting Nuts and Seeds

Store-bought toasted nuts are often heavily salted, so learn to toast your own if you like that roasted flavor. Here is how to do it:

1. Preheat the oven to 350°F (180°C).
2. Toast the nuts whole: if you want to chop them, do it later—tiny pieces of nut burn easily.
3. Toast one type of nut or seed at a time—different nuts have different toasting times.
4. Place your nuts or seeds in a single layer in an ungreased baking sheet.
5. Bake the nuts for five to fifteen minutes until golden. Stir a couple of times during toasting so they brown evenly. Nuts will continue browning a little after they have been removed from the oven, so it is better to under-toast than over-toast them.
6. Remove from the oven and immediately tip onto a plate to cool.
7. When cooled, store in an airtight container in the refrigerator.

Switch It Up

There are countless switches you could make to the trail mix on page 36. For a tropical taste, choose cashews and Brazil nuts, mixed with dried mango, banana chips, and flaked coconut. For a "peanut butter and jelly mix," try peanuts, dried strawberries, and shredded wheat cereal. Or go spicy by mixing your choice of nuts and seeds with a sprinkle of cayenne pepper and garlic powder.

TRAIL MIX

Mix up a batch of this energy-packed trail mix, then store it in an airtight container for up to one month.

You Will Need
1½ cups (210 g) raw nuts, such as almonds, cashews, and peanuts
½ cup (75 g) raw sunflower seeds
½ cup (75 g) raw pumpkin seeds
½ cup (75 g) raisins
½ cup (75 g) dried cranberries
Pinch of cinnamon
Pinch of nutmeg
Pinch of salt (optional)

Instructions
1 If you like the taste of toasted nuts, turn to page 35 to find out how to make them. If you prefer your nuts raw, go straight to step 2.
2 In a large bowl, combine your nuts, seeds, and dried fruit. Mix well, making sure that your fruit is not clumped together.
3 Sprinkle over the cinnamon, nutmeg, and a little salt if you like.
4 Have about ¼ cup (35 g) per snack serving to avoid overdoing it on calories.

Take it on a hike for extra energy!

CHEF'S TIP

Add ½ cup (90 g) of chocolate chips to the mix for a little treat.

SPICY NUTS

Once you start snacking, you will find it hard to stop!

You Will Need

3 tbsp canola oil

3 cups (420 g) mixed nuts, such as almonds, cashews, and Brazil nuts

2 tbsp honey

1 tsp salt

2 tsp ground black pepper

2 tsp cayenne pepper

Instructions

1 Preheat the oven to 280°F (140°C).

2 In a high-sided baking pan, mix together the oil, nuts, honey, and salt.

3 Ensure the nuts are evenly spread in a single layer.

4 Cook for fifteen to twenty minutes, stirring every five minutes, until browned.

5 Remove from the oven and sprinkle the black pepper and cayenne pepper on.

6 Leave to cool, then eat immediately or keep in an airtight container in the refrigerator for up to one month.

cayenne pepper

black pepper

If this recipe is too spicy for you, switch the black and cayenne pepper for 2 tsp of pumpkin pie spice.

CHAPTER 7

FRUIT

As Grandma will tell you, an apple is the best snack you can eat. While you are eating that apple, read on for some ways to add excitement to your fruit bowl.

Two Fruits a Day

Fruit—and vegetables—are vital sources of fiber, minerals, and vitamins. Vitamin C is essential to keep our bodies and immune systems healthy. Vitamin A is important for growth and development and good vision. Is there a downside to fruit? Fruit does contain naturally occurring sugar, or fructose. Fructose in fruit is encased in fiber, which slows down its absorption in our bodies—unlike the "free" sugars found in table sugar, which give us that sugar rush. However, to avoid consuming too much sugar, the United States Department of Agriculture recommends sticking to two servings of fruit per day.

How to Eat Fruit

The choice is yours: eat your fruit fresh, dried, or freeze-dried. Mix it with granola for added carbohydrates (see page 42). If you have more time, bake with fruit to add natural sweetness to muffins or oat bars (see Chapter 5). You could even try stewing fruit by simmering it in a little water until softened.

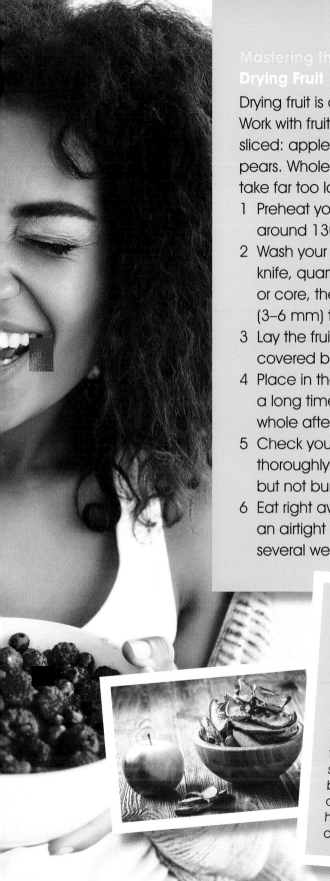

Drying Fruit

Drying fruit is a fun project, with delicious results! Work with fruits that dry well and can be easily sliced: apples, bananas, peaches, plums, or pears. Whole berries (like grapes or strawberries) take far too long to dry. Here is how to do it:

1 Preheat your oven to its lowest setting, around 130–160°F (50–70°C).
2 Wash your fruit thoroughly. Using a sharp knife, quarter each fruit, remove the pit or core, then cut into slices $\frac{1}{8}$ to $\frac{1}{4}$ in (3–6 mm) thick.
3 Lay the fruit in a single layer on a parchment-covered baking sheet.
4 Place in the oven for four to six hours. This is a long time, so you will need to set aside a whole afternoon or evening.
5 Check your fruit regularly. When it is thoroughly dehydrated, it will be shriveled but not burnt.
6 Eat right away, or you can store your fruit in an airtight container in the refrigerator for several weeks.

Switch It Up

If you like the honey and mint dressing for the fruit salad on page 44, try it with different fruits for a change in flavor. How about slicing one apple, one pear, two bananas, three kiwis, and three clementines, then drizzling with honey and mint and the juice of one lime?

RAISIN GRANOLA PARFAIT

Parfait is usually a rich layered dessert, but this one is healthy!

You Will Need

2 cups (200 g) rolled oats
1 tsp ground cinnamon
½ cup (120 ml) apple juice
2 tbsp canola oil
2 tbsp runny honey
1 cup (150 g) raisins
1⅓ cups (320 ml) low-fat plain yogurt

Instructions

1 Preheat the oven to 250°F (120°C).
2 In a large mixing bowl, stir together the oats, cinnamon, apple juice, oil, and honey.
3 Spread the mixture on a baking sheet that has been covered with parchment paper.
4 Bake for fifteen minutes, stirring every few minutes.
5 Stir in the raisins, then bake for another ten to fifteen minutes.
6 Leave your granola to cool.
7 Prepare four bowls of parfait: Put about 4 tbsp yogurt into each bowl, top with 4 tbsp granola—and enjoy.

raisins

CITRUS SALAD

This colorful salad is refreshing and high in vitamin C.

Reserve a few whole mint leaves for a garnish.

You Will Need
4 large oranges
1 pink grapefruit
1 white grapefruit
2 tbsp honey
1 tbsp fresh mint, chopped

Instructions
1 Using your fingers, peel the fruit over a bowl so that you catch the juice. Gently separate each segment. Peel away its skin so you are left with the soft flesh.
2 Place the segments in four bowls.
3 Add the honey and mint to the juice from Step 1, then spoon this mixture over the citrus segments.
4 Eat immediately or refrigerate for an hour or two until you are ready.

mint

CHEF'S TIP
If segmenting the fruit is too time-consuming, peel it with a sharp knife, then slice.

GLOSSARY

baked Cooked in the heat of an oven.

boiling When a liquid is so hot that it releases large bubbles of gas.

bruschetta Toasted Italian bread drenched in olive oil and other toppings, pronounced "broos-ketta."

calories Units used to measure the energy value of food.

carbohydrates Food molecules contained in starchy foods, such as pasta, grains, and potatoes, as well as sugars and fibers, which provide most of your energy.

cilantro The green leaves of the coriander plant.

fiber Long molecules that are contained in plants and help with digestion.

fry Cook in hot oil or fat.

garlic clove One of the sections of a bulb of garlic.

gluten A mixture of two proteins found in cereal grains such as wheat, barley, rye, and some oats.

intolerance An inability to eat a food without having side effects.

kneading Massaging and squeezing dough with the hands.

nutrients Substances found in food that provide essential nourishment for health and growth.

protein A substance found in lentils, beans, nuts, seeds, meat, fish, eggs, and dairy products that is essential for growth and health.

saturated fats Types of "unhealthy" fats that are usually found in animal products such as meat and dairy.

simmer Cook so that the liquid is hot enough to bubble gently but not to boil.

stewed Describes food that has been cooked slowly in liquid.

vegan A person who does not eat any animal products, including eggs, milk products, and honey.

vinaigrette A salad dressing made from oil, vinegar, and seasoning.

whisking Stirring or beating ingredients using the quick movement of a wire utensil, with the aim of introducing air to the mixture.

whole grains Grains obtained from cereal crops, such as wheat, that have not had their nutritious germ (kernel) and bran (outer layer) removed.

wilt Cook very briefly so a leaf becomes limp.

yeast A microscopic fungus used to make bread rise.

FURTHER READING

Books

Ganeshram, Ramin. *FutureChefs: Recipes by Tomorrow's Cooks Across the Nation and the World*. Emmaus, PA: Rodale Books, 2014.

Huff, Lisa. *Kid Chef Bakes*. Emeryville, CA: Rockridge Press, 2017.

Kuskowski, Alex. *Cool Healthy Muffins: Fun & Easy Baking Recipes for Kids!* Minneapolis, MN: ABDO Publishing Company, 2015.

Parker, Vic. *Snacks*. Chicago, IL: Heinemann Library, 2014.

Websites

Healthy Snacks for Teens
teens.webmd.com/features/healthy-snacks-for-teens
Find out about the nutritional value of snacks.

Quick and Easy Snack Recipes
www.foodnetwork.com/healthy/photos/quick-and-easy-snack-recipes
Get more easy snack inspiration.

Smart Snacking
kidshealth.org/en/teens/healthy-snacks.html
Read this article all about healthy snacking.

Top 8 Healthy Snacks for Teens
www.superhealthykids.com/top-8-healthy-snacks-teenagers
This is a great website with lots of healthy snack ideas.

INDEX